Jesus Wept

Presented to

_____

by

_____

_____

_____

_____, 19_____

Other Brownlow Gift Books

Jesus Wept

TRUSTING THE
GOOD SHEPHERD
WHEN YOU LOSE
A LOVED ONE

LEROY BROWNLOW

BROWNLOW PUBLISHING CO., INC.
FORT WORTH, TEXAS

Printed in the United States of America.

ISBN 0-915720-12-4

CONTENTS

CHAPTER ONE

"COMFORT ONE ANOTHER WITH THESE WORDS"

When our loved one is taken from us, we suffer the agony of having a part of ourselves cut in two. It is then that we weep from hearts that bleed like "a vine bleeds when a green branch is cut from it."

Our suffering is then, as Longfellow stated, "the common fate of all"; for "into each life some rain must fall." But if there were no raindrops, there would be no rainbows in the heavens; and if there were no teardrops, there would be no rainbows in the soul. Sorrow often mellows and beautifies the soul like the night's dew gives the rose its deepest hue.

Out of sorrow the sweetest souls have emerged. The most sympathetic hearts are marked with scars from wounds which have healed. We never get too big to cry. Tears often come from a bigness of heart that has to have relief. Like water spills over from a vessel filled beyond its capacity, tears will flow from a heart that can hold no more.

There are times when tears befit and beautify us all.

Sorrow is as universal as man. Its pangs make no exceptions. And the cry for help is just as universal as the hurt. "Help me! Help me!" And just as long as people hurt, they will cry out for a cure. However the centuries have taught humanity that the lasting cure for heart pain is not in medication but in meditation. That determines what we are and what we become—distressed or consoled. "For as he thinketh in his heart, so is he" (Proverbs 23:7).

Comfort is found in words. Knowing this, the Apostle Paul said, "Wherefore comfort one another with these words" (I Thessalonians 4:18). Comfort in words. That's where you find it: in words, in words which convey the healing thoughts.

So let us think upon a few precious meditations—not new ones but old ones—almost as old as the hills and more enduring; rational reflections tested by the centuries; gleaming thoughts of comfort which have for ages penetrated man's night of despair in a dark world of misunderstanding, made still darker by a fog of doubt.

It was David, the ancient shepherd boy, who skillfully and pictorially expressed the hope of frail man in the eloquent and immortal Twenty-third Psalm. For hundreds of years, on every shore and in every clime, it has dried the tears and healed the hearts of countless numbers who helplessly stood by and watched as husband or wife, son or daughter, father or mother, brother or sister slipped down through the valley of the shadow of death. Its words have been upon the trembling lips of millions who slowly turned from the flower-decked mound where the earthly frame they loved so dearly was placed to sleep in hallowed ground. And later, when time stood still in mournful shadows, as they tried to put back together a broken heart, they found peace in the way of life and death provided by the Good Shepherd. Today man's needs are no different.

The shepherd's psalm is still a balm for hearts that ache and bleed and break.

CHAPTER TWO

"THE LORD IS MY SHEPHERD"

The Shepherd Hymn

The Lord is my shepherd;
I shall not want.
He maketh me to lie down in green pastures:
He leadeth me beside the still waters.
He restoreth my soul:
He leadeth me in the paths of
*   righteousness for his name's sake.*
Yea, though I walk through the valley
*   of the shadow of death,*
I will fear no evil; for thou art with me:
Thy rod and thy staff, they comfort me.
Thou preparest a table before me
*   in the presence of mine enemies:*
Thou anointest my head with oil;
My cup runneth over.
Surely goodness and mercy shall
*   follow me all the days of my life:*
And I will dwell in the house
*   of the Lord for ever.*

Picture ourselves in the Orient. The sun is radiant-hot. The earth is scorched dry. We see a few wobbly sheep nibbling at burnt grass already bitten too close to the disappointing ground. Sheep without food, without water, without future. Wait a moment! Not so fast! There is more to the picture. Our view broadens, and we see the shepherd standing nearby. His existence is as real as the sheep. And his presence, power, and providence change the entire outlook.

In pastoral eloquence, David confidently said, "The Lord is my shepherd."

There is no explanation for either life or matter apart from a first cause, a starting point. Something self-existent had to exist first from which everything else has come. This is the flawless conclusion from unerring logic. For instance: Something cannot come from nothing, but something is; therefore something always was. And that something that always was and is and shall be is God, the Eternal Spirit, the Good Shepherd. He was David's Shepherd, and he is mine. The actuality of his existence—no myth— enlarges the perspective for man, which gives us courage in life and consolation in death.

In complete trust, David continues, "I shall not want."

The shepherd calls and the struggling sheep, in an effort to follow, muster the last full measure of devotion in the giving of the last fading ounce of strength. They do not know where they are going, but they know the shepherd. That is enough. They trust him. Each has the assurance: "I shall not want."

The journey commences. Clouds of dust form and hang over them in choking discomfort.

> *The shepherd has information not possessed by the sheep. Their knowledge is so limited. But he knows beyond the hills there is a valley where life is pleasant.*

There are rocks to avoid for fear that famished sheep will stumble never to arise. There are holes to bypass; otherwise spindling legs may be mortally entrapped. There are thorns stretching out to cut and tear; so a detour is in order. But on they go—laboriously—wending their way down the hill, adjusting themselves to the conditions along the trail.

At last they arrive in the valley of plenty. The shepherd has supplied their needs. The sheep who had nothing without him now have

15

everything with him. They are truly blessed.

They "lie down in green pastures beside still waters."

They eat and are satisfied. They drink without fear, for the shepherd has led them away from the rushing, roaring current to where the water is still. There is quiet without and peace within.

The shepherd has restored them. He has led them in the paths of goodness for his name's sake.

But don't think there have been no dangers or ordeals. However, in spite of both, they feared no evil. Life without fear! And for one reason and for one reason only—the presence of the shepherd! That made the difference. That was the source of their security.

So—David, once a shepherd, used this nerve-quieting imagery to describe his own relationship to his own Shepherd and to account for his own life without fear. His confidence in the Shepherd of all shepherds gave him a gallantry

Fear has been replaced with comfort. "Thy rod and thy staff they comfort me." Comfort! One of our most crying needs and David found it—not through his own power, but through the power of the Good Shepherd.

16

marked and made famous by this heroic declaration: *"I will fear no evil: for thou art with me."*
That's why—"thou art with me."

The lowly sheep are favored with a prepared
table. "Thou preparest a table before me in the
presence of mine enemies." Wild animals encir-
cle them. They growl and howl, but keep their
distance. They dare not come any closer, knowing they would have to fight the shepherd. The
sheep enjoy protection because they have a pro-
tector; and this makes life good, though there
are enemies.

Now the day is nearly over. The rose-tinted
hues of sunset quickly fade into twilight. At last
comes the night. And as the evening shadows
lengthen, the shepherd manifests more mercy.
He has provided a fold or an enclosure, and at
the door he stands and personally greets all who
enter. *He anoints every head with oil and quenches
every thirst with a cup of cold water,* brim-full and
running over, as extra benefactions.

Then the door of the fold is barred. The
sheep are as safe in the night as in the day.
They sleep in peace. Assurance is their fortune
and hope is their benediction.

David sums up the pastoral in ascribing to

17

Forever! There is no end. What we call the end is only transition—just a new beginning.

his own feelings this poetic declaration of poise: *"Surely goodness and mercy shall follow me all the days of my life: and I will dwell in the house of the Lord for ever."*

> *There is no death! What seems so*
> *is transition:*
> *This life of mortal breath*
> *Is but a suburb of the life elysian,*
> *Whose portal we call death.*
>
> —Henry W. Longfellow

CHAPTER THREE

"IN MY FATHER'S HOUSE ARE MANY MANSIONS"

A move from one house to another does not end the life of the tenant. When this old house—this body—shall have broken down, man shall be given a fairer dwelling made for eternity.

The Tenant

This body is my house—it is not I;
Herein I sojourn till, in some far sky,
I lease a fairer dwelling, built to last
Till all the carpentry of time is past.
(In a new house away from) this lone star,
What shall I care where these
    poor timbers are?
What, though the crumbling walls
    turn dust and loam—
I shall have left them for a larger home.

—Frederick Lawrence Knowles

Fashioned by a mighty hand that does all things well, our new bodies, made to last world without end, shall never know harassment and

19

hurt, sickness and sorrow, despair and death; for the Great Giver shall design them to be like his own glorious body. For the Bible, in speaking of our Lord, says, "Who shall change our vile body, that it may be fashioned like unto his glorious body, according to the working whereby he is able even to subdue all things unto himself" (Philippians 3:21).

It is in this triumphant faith that we live in the sooth-ing solace that only a part of us shall ever die.

The Bible says: "For we know that if our earthly house of this tabernacle were dissolved, we have a building of God, a house not made with hands, eternal in the heavens" (II Corinthians 5:1).

In speaking of another house de-signed to last forever, our Lord once said: "Let not your heart be troubled [sorrowful but not troubled]: ye believe in God, believe also in me. In my Father's house are many mansions: if it were not so, I would have told you. I go to prepare a place for you [it is a reality]. And if I go and pre-pare a place for you, I will come again, and receive you unto myself; that where I am, there ye may be also" (John 14:1-3).

We can trust the Good Shepherd! For he has said, "Where I am, there ye may be also."

20

In My Father's House

No, not cold beneath the grasses,
Not close-walled within the tomb;
Rather, in our Father's mansion,
Living in another room.
Shall I doubt my Father's mercy?
Shall I think of death as doom,
Or the stepping o'er the threshold
To a bigger, brighter room?
Shall I blame my Father's wisdom?
Shall I sit enswathed in gloom,
When I know my loves are happy—
Waiting, in another room?

—Robert Freeman

How precious is the thought of another room over there in the land fairer than earth.

The hope of a new house in a new habitation has been the longing of men through the ages. Abraham's quest has been their deep and abiding concern. "For he looked for a city which hath foundations whose builder and maker is God" (Hebrews 11:10).

In meditating on the blossoming rose and the graceful vine that bore it, we discover an artistic lesson on immortality.

For a running rose to find a crevice in the wall

21

and to pass through and to bloom on the other side does not stop it from living.

To our departed we say: Death hides but not divides; beloved, you are on the other side.

The Rose Still Grows Beyond the Wall

Near a stony wall a rose once grew,
    Budded and blossomed in God's free light;
Watered and fed by morning dew,
    Shedding its sweetness day and night.

As it grew and blossomed fair and tall,
    Slowly rising to loftier height,
It came to a crevice in the wall
    Through which there shone
        a beam of light.

Onward it crept with added strength,
    With no fear to face the sharp divide;
It followed the light through
        the crevice-length,
And unfolded itself on the other side.

The light, the dew, the broadening view,
    Were found better than they were before;
And it lost itself in beauties new,
    Scattering its fragrance more and more.

Shall claim of death cause us to grieve,
    And make our courage faint or fall?
Nay, let us faith and hope receive,—
    Man ever lives beyond the wall,—

23

Breathing fragrance far and wide,
Just as he did in days of yore;
Just as he did on the earthly side;
Just as he will forevermore.

—Adapted, A. L. Frink

We should not think that a ship which sails
beyond our sight has become lost. Every sea must
have another shore, and it is natural that people
live there as well as here. When a ship passes
that line where water and sky blend in one
embrace, it has only voyaged farther from us
and closer to those who wait its coming on the
faraway shore. In sorrow we say, "It is gone." In
joy they shout, "It is here."

What is it like o'er there to be,
Home for the sailor, home from the sea?

It leaves us wondering how very fair it must
be over there; and in quest of knowledge which
this world can never fully reveal, we strain our
eyes in search of light along the distant shore.

But our vision is too short to scan the scene.
It is not yet ours to see—rather it is now ours to
believe.

So—as unknown waves before me roll, I'm
left to a journey of faith in the Eternal Pilot to

guide me over life's tempestuous sea.

> *So, on I go, not knowing*
> *I would not, if I might.*
> *I would rather sail in the dark with God*
> *Than sail alone in the light.*
> *I would rather sail with Him by faith,*
> *Than sail alone by sight.*
>
> —Mary G. Brainard

And then when faith turns into sight, we shall see for ourselves:

> *What must it be to step on shore,*
> *and find it—Heaven;*
> *To take hold of a hand,*
> *and find it—God's hand;*
> *To breathe a new air*
> *and find it—Celestial air;*
> *To feel invigorated,*
> *and find it—Immortality;*
> *To sail from the care and turmoil of earth*
> *To one unbroken calm;*
> *To land there and find it—Glory.*

For school to be out merely closes the classes— not the life of the student. It rather gives him a chance to rest from his studies and to enjoy his learning. So goes life in a world designed to be a preparatory school. In it we learn from many

25

sources. And after the learner has finished his course, it is only natural for him to go home.

When School Is Out

Why be afraid of death,
as though your life were breath?
Death but anoints your eyes with clay.
O glad surprise!

Why should it be a wrench
to leave your wooden bench,
Why not with happy shout
run home when school is out?

This is the death of Death,
to breathe away a breath
And know the end of strife,
and taste the deathless life,
And joy without a fear,
and smile without a tear,
And work, nor care to rest,
and find the last the best.

—Maltbie D. Babcock

The last must be the best. It is too necessary not to be true. Another life is essential to the continuation of the Creator's work. The world turns and toils for the good of man. All plant life and all creature life exist for his benefit. Day and night succeed each other. The seasons come and go. Vegetation springs out of the earth to go back to the earth again. Animals are born, live and perish in the fulfillment of a plan.

Now if this is the fate of man—in one word, if man has only a vegetable or animal existence—then what is gained by the whole operation? What does the Creator accomplish? If man is lost, forever lost, all is lost. If heaven is only a myth, then nature is only a maze of foolish nonsense in which man is merely a monstrous miscarriage and a colossal calamity. Unthinkable! Man's imperishability is far too essential to be false.

He will not leave our treasures
    in the dust,
For God is just.
    NECESSITATION!

The hope sublime
    that soared into the sky,—
Can such hope die? NO!

The faith serene
    that smiled at death—
Was it but breath? NO!

The hand that fashioned man has not dropped in weakness to deathly failure, but to the contrary has lifted itself in power to deathless heights—to heaven. It has to be so!

27

The love that served and took
   no thought of cost,—
Can it be lost? NO!

Nay, is it not with forces such as these
God peoples His eternities? YES!

—Adapted, Charles Carroll Albertson

Therefore, we insist:

"Earth to earth, and dust to dust"
Necessitates another must—
   It was not spoken of the soul.

Solomon said it this way: "Then shall the dust return to the earth as it was: and the spirit shall return unto God who gave it" (Ecclesiastes 12:7).

29

"YE SHALL FIND REST UNTO YOUR SOULS"

Don't be ashamed to weep. For it is sweet sorrow that grieves in hope. There is nothing as beautiful as the smile of expectation which breaks through the tears of sorrow. Thank God, there is less hurt in the grief influenced by the belief that we shall be reunited beyond the fading hills. For this reason—and understandably—the Bible says, "...that ye sorrow not, even as others which have no hope" (I Thessalonians 4:13). So the mourning is actually for ourselves.

> *Not for him but for us*
> *should our tears be shed;*
> *Mourn, mourn, for the living,*
> *but not for the dead.*

There is consolation, but still the heart aches. "Consolation implies rather an augmentation of the power of bearing than a diminution of the burden." Though we sorrow for ourselves, it is still sorrow and it hurts; and as an outlet, we weep and it helps. It is a law of nature.

This is a land of smiles and tears, and as we pass through it we are visited with both. It is comforting, therefore, to know that your beloved has ended this pilgrimage where joy often turns to sorrow. Having completed the journey, your love has moved over there where "God shall wipe away all tears; and there shall be no more death, neither sorrow, nor crying, neither shall there be any more pain; for the former things are passed away" (Revelation 21:4).

Don't blame yourself. Of course, there were times when you were a little neglectful, impatient, inconsiderate, and maybe rude. But that's human. No person can live in the flesh without being subject to the weaknesses of the flesh. Don't censure yourself for being human. All have fallen short in some respects. "For all have sinned, and come short of the glory of God" (Romans 3:23).

God forgives and forgets. So should you.

It is better to remember the special moments, days, weeks, and years of soothing smoothness, the pleasantness too sweet to put in human speech. No one can take from you those precious memories.

In those never-to-be-forgotten recollections, your loved one lives, and to linger in hearts that remember is not to die.

Don't think that God has called your loved one home to punish you. Life is filled with whys, and sometimes the wrong ones are asked out of misunderstanding. Why has God thus dealt with me? Why is God disciplining me so severely? What have I done to deserve such punishment? These questions (and many more) reveal a hurt, a perplexity and a misunderstanding of sorrow. They come from a narrow view of the Creator's design of life and death. They originate in a misinterpretation of the Father's plan for the *now* and the *hereafter.*

He considers the welfare of the dying as well as the living; and His calling one home is not to hurt us who remain, but to help him who departs.

God has a concern for the one he beckons home as well as for the one he leaves behind.

When your loved one's work on earth was finished, there was no course left for him or her but to move into a more blessed realm where more beautiful services can be performed forever. For it is there that "...his servants shall serve him: And

32

they shall see his face..." (Revelation 22:3, 4).

Life's earthly relationships continually teach us to give up a loved one and share him or her in a higher place. Parents are called upon to allow their children to leave the home nest so they may make a love nest for themselves. Although the separation is painful, joy is found in the self-denying love that wants the child to have the fuller life. When our friends are called to higher jobs in faraway places, we say good-bye in the hope that we shall meet again. We never accuse the corporation of calling them just to punish us. Why then should we misunderstand the call of God?

Life is full of separations, but love is full of sacrifices. The same principle of love "that seeketh not its own" should be applied to the separation necessitated when the Good Shepherd calls. It should heroically accept the personal loss on the wider basis that all is well for me here that is better for him or her over there. This is the unselfish view of death. This is the heroics of a love that does not count my grief more than I consider his or her relief.

All of this adds up to acceptance. Refusing to let go of the *might-have-beens* will not change

33

the *haves,* the *nows,* and the *must-bes.* What has happened is as real as yesterday. *The reality of the now is as factual as today.* And what must be is as real as tomorrow. And the sooner you accept realism—and without resentment—the sooner your life can settle down to the regular living God expects of you.

Solomon said, "Man goeth to his long home, and the mourners go about the streets" (Ecclesiastes 12:5). So—"go about the streets." *Don't run away from those streets.* Don't hide. Go back to your tasks and duties. Your life has not ended. So—don't assign to yourself a breathing death, a life in which you breathe but don't live.

There's too much to live for to die before your time. It's your lot to live.

It's your duty to be brave. It's your obligation to carry on as you did before. So—pick up your paint brush and keep on painting your dreams on the canvas of life.

There is no disrespect in this to the departed. It rather respects your loved one by respecting the life and the courage that he or she had to live it.

A young husband and father suffered an accident which took his life. The shock of such an unexpected passing left the wife stunned and

34

heartbroken. The blow had staggered her, but after a few days she was able to reach down into the bottom of her soul and come up with the valor which began to sustain her. She knew she had to carry on. Her husband had liked company and coffee. So—she invited some of their old friends to the home. She said to them, "Do come. I think, through the ear of faith, I can hear John say, 'Atta girl, keep that welcome mat out and that coffee pot on the stove.'" She was right in doing this. To have locked herself and her children behind dark walls of grief would hurt only herself and them. He would not have wanted it that way.

Christian philosophy includes both living and dying. Now is the time to live. The latter will come soon enough.

It was in the evening of life that Dr. Robert J. Burdette, a minister, wrote in a personal letter:

> "For me to live is Christ, and to die is gain" (Philippians 1:21).

"My work is about ended, I think. The best of it I have done poorly; any of it I might have done better, but I have done it. And in a fairer land, with finer material and a better working light, I will do better." He had learned acceptance—and hope.

35

AND THAT
IS DYING

Death is only the cut-
ting of a delicate flower that enables it to bloom
anew in an eternal garden more beautiful and
fragrant than earth's eye has ever beheld.

> *Catch, then, O catch the transient hour;*
> *Improve each moment as it flies;*
> *Life's a short summer—man a flower.*
>
> —Samuel Johnson

That is dying.

Another analogy which explains the transistory
effect of death is the seed. The Bible says, "That
which thou sowest is not quickened, except it
die" (I Corinthians 15:36). The secret of life
enclosed in the seed cannot be developed until
the seed has died. So the blessed and eternal possibilities for human beings cannot be realized
until these earthly bodies have died and gone
the way of all mortal flesh. The explanation in
the Bible continues, "It is sown in corruption; it

is raised in incorruption...it is sown in weakness; it is raised in power: it is sown a natural body; it is raised a spiritual body" (I Corinthians 15:42-44). It is as the Holy Bible has stated: "We shall be changed.... For this corruptible must put on incorruption, and this mortal must put on immortality" (I Corinthians 15:52, 53).

It would be the human family's worst tragedy if man could not die or be transformed. It would deny him of unlimited possibilities in another habitation which defy earthly description and finite understanding.

As the little seed is required to die before it can live in its final and most lovely form, man too must die before he can attain the highest and most blessed state of life. If God has the power in nature to bring forth a brighter and more beautiful life from the dead seed buried in mother earth, then we should not doubt his power to clothe our souls with new bodies, suited to a new existence in a better world when these bodies lie in earth's hallowed soil.

God meant that man's shedding one body to be clothed with another will be only a lying down to pleasant dreams.

So live that, when thy summons
    comes to join
The innumerable caravan which moves
To that mysterious realm where
    each shall take
His chamber in the silent halls of death,
Thou go not like the quarry slave at night
Scourged to his dungeon; but,
    sustained and soothed
By an unfaltering trust, approach thy grave
Like one who wraps the drapery of his couch
About him and lies down
    to pleasant dreams.
                    —*Thanatopsis,* William Cullen Bryant

That is dying.

Death was appointed to emancipate us, give us
freedom from a world of sin and sorrow, rebellion and regret. This liberation, death, is one of
the most precious blessings of God. Death is not
the blighting curse that some
have supposed, but a blessed
necessity made possible by the
love and wisdom of God.

> "Precious in
> the sight of
> the Lord is
> the death
> of his saints"
> (Psalms 116:15).

After God created Adam and
Eve, he placed them in the Garden
of Eden and imposed a law upon them, which
they deliberately broke. Sin dwelt in the land.

39

There was the downfall of the human family. It would not be in man's good interest to live forever in a state of lawlessness, rebellion and transgression. Something had to be done to liberate man from such a state. So mercy was extended to our first parents by our Father's driving them out of the garden before they could "take also of the tree of life, and eat, and live forever" (Genesis 3:22-24). Separation from the tree of life brought death.

Leaving the tree of life here in the first part of the Bible, we never find it mentioned again until we come to the last book in the Bible, Revelation. There it is mentioned in connection with another beautiful garden, heaven itself, and those who enter may eat of the tree of life and live forever in a state of perfect submission. When this comes to pass, man's emancipation will have been completed and perfected.

That is dying.

Death was appointed to effect the transition from mortality to immortality. It is a departure of the soul. In speaking of Rachel's death the Bible says, "And it came to pass, as her soul was in departing, (for she died)" (Genesis 35:18). This is possible because of the dual nature of man.

Solomon said, "Then shall the dust return to the earth as it was: and the spirit shall return unto God who gave it" (Ecclesiastes 12:7). Prompted by love, God designed death to be an exit from this world and an entrance into another world. It is the going home. When our life on earth is ended and our sun of time has set, it is then that a new life will dawn upon us and a new day will rise forever more.

At End

At end of view, at end of life,
At end of hope, at end of strife,
At end of all we cling to so,
The sun is setting—must we go?

At dawn of view, at dawn of life,
At dawn of peace that follows strife,
At dawn of all we long for so,
The sun is rising—let us go.

—Louise Chandler Moulton

That is dying.

We must of necessity leave "our earthly house of this tabernacle" because "flesh and blood cannot inherit the kingdom of God" (II Corinthians

41

5:1; I Corinthians 15:50). These bodies are not suited to a spiritual and eternal habitation. In death, we shed the corruptible body that we may become incorruptible. "This mortal must put on immortality." This is the way "death is swallowed up in victory." It is over there that man's soul will be clothed with a new body "like unto his glorious body" (Philippians 3:21). This will adapt us to an everlasting life. With immortal bodies and sinless living, nothing will ever mar the peace and happiness of those who enter heaven. There no storm clouds will ever rise. There we shall not be dead—just away.

That is dying.

Likewise from the earthly viewpoint, we can see the blessing of death. In our world as we know it, death is an essential requirement of life. Suppose no living thing should ever die. Suppose that in the animal kingdom, animals are born and multiply and never die. Suppose that in plant life, plants live and multiply, but not one ever dies. Suppose that in the human family, people live and continue to live, multiply and continue to multiply, but no one ever tastes of death. We see that life would soon become unbearable.

42

Death is a prerequisite of life. What a friend we have in death—all our afflictions lose their hold. Suppose the aged could only become older, the distressed could only suffer more agony and the suffering could only hurt more intensely—and nobody could die. There would be no future in this. Then living would be a thousand times worse than dying; for the Christian's death is loss only to those who linger behind.

For those who remain on this side of the chasm of time, death is loss; but for those who have crossed over, it is gain.

It is only our shortsighted and temporal view of life that dims our appreciation of death. But having entered "that bourn from which no traveler returns," it is then that ten thousand celestial glories which defy the tongue of any orator to describe will burst on our enraptured vision, and we shall see them as they really are.

A few years ago I went with my father to Houston, Texas, where he underwent very critical surgery in which the chances of living, barring divine help, were not in his favor. However, God was gracious to him and to us; he did survive and lived seven years.

43

The night before the operation, as others were leaving the room, he requested that I remain for awhile. He wanted to discuss some business and personal matters. When the discussion was concluded, as I prepared to leave, he took me by the hand and said, "Son, if I come through in the morning, it will be just wonderful; if I don't, it will still be all right." Though he had but little formal schooling, I believe the words were well put and the statement is deep and profound. This is the philosophy of life and death which God intends for us to have. If I live through tomorrow, it will be just wonderful; if I don't, it will still be all right. This is the way to live, and this is the way to die. "To live is Christ, and to die is gain." We know not the future, but we know God is in it. This means all is well.

Despite all the blessings God has provided in death, it still turns our eyes into fountains of tears when our loved ones are called home. Staggering beneath our loss, tottering beneath a burden that seems too heavy, conscious that our shattered world must be put back together some way, somehow, without the missing part, our mournful hearts cry out for help. "Help us." How old are these words; yet they are the

anguished plea of each new generation.

Nature itself has provided help—tears. It is natural that we weep, just as natural as it is for the birds to sing, for the flowers to bloom, for the oceans to have water and for the mountains to be tall. Birds are supposed to sing, flowers were made to bloom, oceans naturally contain water and mountains are naturally tall; and human beings, created in the image of God, are naturally formed to feel and be touched with grief when death separates them from their loved ones. This is a natural reaction because we are the offspring of God, not animals.

"Jesus wept" (John 11:35) is the shortest verse in the Bible. In the light of this, we have never told sorrowful pilgrims with swollen eyes who look through their tears for a glimpse of life along the distant shore not to weep.

He understands your tears.

Sometimes when we feel that a volcano of distress will erupt within us, we find relief only through our tears. Just as the rainbow is formed only through tears of nature, we too are permitted to see the world in all of its colors only through our

> *Tears are not only acceptable and normal, but they can be sacred, for "Jesus wept."*

tears. Paul said, "Rejoice with them that do rejoice, and weep with them that weep" (Romans 12:15). This is the Christian spirit.

But we want more relief than tears can afford. We want something more satisfying than just weeping until we can weep no more. We crave a consolation that will dry up our tears and heal our heart. Thanks be to God, he has repeatedly reasoned with us in the realm of logic and consoled us in the field of promise, as pointed out in the chapter.

Certainly there is nothing more comforting than the thought of continuing life forever in the eternal city of many mansions. Jesus used it to expel trouble and fear from the hearts of his close associates. Shortly before he died for a lost and bankrupt world, he said to those disciples who were soon to be scattered as sheep without a shepherd: "Let not your heart be troubled; ye believe in God, believe also in me. In my Father's house are many mansions."

And that is dying.